# The Inward Gaze

## Radiance of Inner Illumination

Vijay Srinivas

/ BookLeaf Publishing

India | USA | UK

Made with ❤ on the BookLeaf Publishing Platform
www.bookleafpub.in
www.bookleafpub.com

# Dedication

*To*

## *Appa*

## *&*

## *Amma*

# Preface

Poetry is the silent dialogue of the soul, a gentle conversation between the inner light and the quiet shadows that shape our being. This collection, *The Inward Gaze* - Radiance of Inner Illumination, is born from long walks through the corridors of the mind, from moments of reflection that whispered the truths too tender for everyday speech.

This collection can also be a journey into the heart of Tamil classical poetry—Venba—a form renowned for its harmony between meter, meaning, and meter's musicality. Though these poems began as Tamil venbas, their English versions herein are not mere translations but rebirths—crafted to carry the essence, emotions, and beauty of the originals into a new language and culture. Though rooted in the classical traditions of Venba, yet breathing with contemporary feelings, this book is a bridge between time and self — a tapestry woven from threads of moments that linger,touch,radiate and breathe.

Each poem is a self-contained universe of feeling and reflection, shaped by centuries of Tamil literary tradition yet breathing in present-day poetic sensibility. Without the Tamil text, these verses stand independently as lyrical explorations of inner light, resilience, love,affection, and the human spirit's enduring landscapes. It is my hope that readers who encounter these poems find not only a window into Tamil poetic heritage but also an intimate companion for their own inner journeys.

In these verses, I have sought to capture the delicate dance of emotions, the steadfastness of silent strength, and the luminous hope embedded in human resilience. Each poem is a doorway — sometimes a subtle gaze, sometimes a resounding call — inviting readers to journey inward, to uncover the unseen landscapes where dreams meet reality, and where the heart's quiet wisdom blooms. Let these verses resonate with your own story, illuminating new paths within and beyond.

Thank you for opening these pages and walking with me through this illuminated path.

—

# Acknowledgements

This book grew not from plans or pages, but from lived fragments — moments when silence pressed too close, and words found a way through the seams. It owes its existence to the untidy, unpredictable theater of life that whispered, protested, and consoled in turns.

To the *trifles* — the unremarked coffee steam, the falling leaf, the echo of footsteps in late corridors — thank you for teaching patience without ever speaking.

To the *afternoons* that blurred into rain, the *nights* that refused rest, and the *dawns* that bargained with hope, you were all lessons in being human.

To the *joys* that came quietly, to the *pains* that arrived uninvited yet stayed as mentors, to the *mistakes* that softened the spirit, and to the small *mercies* that stitched it whole again — every one of you carved a verse.

And to *every unseen hand*, every *ordinary day*, and every *fleeting face* that passed and stayed somewhere within memory's field — you are the unnamed chorus of this book.

In the end, these poems are not acknowledgements —they are returns.

**To life, in all its imperfection and grace.**

# Pathway into Awakening

A gaze drops dew — an earnest start,
 each day moistens fresh, a gleaming verse.
 Emotion flows, the language of life;
 Silence itself unfolds the path ahead.

Endless flow — the compass finds its meaning,
 roots awaken the eye's clear sight.
 True shadow is a steady grace;
 The light that spills foster an empathizing heart.

A world spun by pure words —
 though illusion hides, love roots in earth.
 Brave hearts bear the sacred flame,
 blossoming like honeyed light in fire.

Desire is flame; when the wind speaks,
 time unveils the eager scene.
 Vision sharpens, paths reveal,
 the shadow of will takes root and lives.

The mind's gaze paints daily scenes —
 on silent trails softly traced,
 meanings shift beyond known frames,
 within, ourselves reborn afresh.

# Chords of Silence and Shade

The darkness in dream dims —
 as light falls, tears dry away,
 even the darkest night gifts sky;
 Understanding births true meaning.

What moves each day, unseen by us —
 time's circle glows in humble turn.
 In truth's light blossoms awareness rare;
 Solitude refines with silent grace.

Hidden beside the silent hush —
 sound swirls, becoming whispered words.
 Blessings pour from ancient tongues;
 The moment, even the direction craves an ear.

Movements stir within the inner chamber —
 A melody melting into memory's fold.
 Not love, but poet's gentle steps;
 Where feeling's edge gives rise to grace.

Traces return in cycles —
 new paths are etched with familiar lines.
 One sign appears again and again;
 Knowing it, does the way not settle?

# Harmonic Silhouettes

When the parrot speaks, rebellion fills the air —
branches and trees bewilder the mind,
A rhythm-less music surfaces;
O heart, learn this discordant part.

In shadows' pace, a tender motion —
mind and time imprint on earth,
vision anew births still in absence of Light;
O eye, acts as reflexive.

Within the treasury's frame a faint sound —
fading in the cooling mind,
beauty dwells as hidden music;
O Mind, Spread that chillness everywhere.

Silent rivers seek new courses —
starry poems flood like waves,
mind light circles the sand's horse;
O upcoming turn, give a moment of clarity.

Traces return in cycles —
new paths are etched with familiar lines.
One sign appears again and again;
O Knowing, does the way not settle?

# The Heart and Wonders

Rare are those who grasp self with self-aligned —
 leading ahead, bearing few days' weights,
 walking behind is the penance that stays true —
 that state, my heart, is where I belong.

We journey each moment, sleep and dew aside,
 A step of fortune's swift embrace,
 we walk the tread with kindly faults —
 shadow and true step, heart alive.

In thoughts, anxiety flows like flood,
 binding ties, melting unheard truths,
 darkness falls and grips my eye —
 here comes strain, heart bends away.

Letting go is easy; holding on is hard —
 burden pressed, heart entwined in pain,
 steadily enduring, standing as a ray —
 living a victory, heart of strain.

Few hearts betray no deceit —
 in softness, smiles like dawn,
 the heart is a language of signs —
 pure souls near pain's edge speak without words.

# Guiding Dreams

An inner light opens in silent space—
  on known old roads, a sudden unknown trace,
  it gathers all, needing never word;
  Such begins a new thought's grace.

Removing the barrier from the eye that looks ahead,
  in rising dawn's harmonious light it comes,
  humanness moves in moments of beauty—
  guiding dreams like a graceful flame.

Moments throw verses with poetic edge,
  A deep shade like a pupil's core,
  melting fusion in mingled thoughts—
  guiding dreams as shimmering heat.

Life stands on the path where light strays,
  A slope where senses gently nudge,
  A burden condenses in spitting heat—
  radiant light, guide dreams anew.

Among a thousand memories, one shade remains,
  seeking conversation on a melting path,
  one melding sound of deep feeling—
  A guiding dream as a ringing voice.

# Enchanting Gateways

The treasury gate opens wide in rhyme,
 like melting veins of silver time,
 through dreams arise new thoughts awake—
 a door that guides the soul to climb.

A solitary breeze untouched yet softly felt,
 arrives from far with quiet melt;
 Where melting thoughts in purity reside,
 A dream's own tone becomes the guide.

Drops adorn the green's return,
 A humbled heart at doorways learns,
 its echo breathes a fragrant drift—
 A dream that walks, a journey's gift.

Emotions trace the path of life,
 they breathe in pause, beyond the strife,
 unknown becomes the known again—
 to feel is truth, to move is gain.

Memories flow as waters run,
 glimpses gleam beneath the sun—
 if knowing filled the soul complete,
 unknowing still would sing its beat.

# Inner Depths of Love

Living with the stains, wisdom's embrace,
the moonlit trust of world on love's grace,
love's Garden a balm for all pain—
do you perceive this essence, O world?

Inner peace like the lotus pure,
calm descended as divine grace,
sweetness flutters on gentle wings—
do you see this guise, O world?

Two sharp words ease burdened hearts,
no long speech or drawn-out parts,
moment's taste felt only by the soul—
do you understand this depth, O world?

Those who sought chances lived, they say,
truth bears no fame on its way,
unfaltering, flows like eternal streams—
do you honour them, O world?

Truth shines though it falls into falsehood,
there was never a time it failed to glow,
the light of reality marks birth anew—
do you grasp this shade, O world?

# Inner Life and Trails

In thoughts where old time has left its trace,
 words blossom to quench hungry flames,
 A dear voice's roar lost through distant times—
 can you tune this frequency, O world?

In forward chance, vision struggles bright,
 behind, false bounds change nature's might,
 balance shifts within the field of moments—
 can you know this hardship, O world?

Soft sounds where quiet thought prevails,
 what lives behind mind's distant trails,
 locked behind closed doors of vanished dreams —
 can you see me dissolve, O world?

In dark turmoil, a simple light shines,
an image appears grand and gifting,
brain wave shows thought's soft glow—
 can you perceive the overview, O world?

One who rises beyond the flesh,
 steadfast, skillful, begins with zeal,
 who dares strive from start to end?
 Can you see their trials, O world?

# The Unyielding State

In gatherings advancing, the humble voice spoke,
 self-uprising fell like a shadow—O elder,
 should not true conduct shine like moonlight?
 Do many understand, O world?

Illness dwells alone within itself,
 the pushing foot's time endures—reflection,
 do those fallen know? Do the coming ones feel?
 Does the burden carried honored, O world?

In groups, steadfast steps unyielding,
 living unshaken they changed the world—
 those who swam with heart in flood,
 don't their values acknowledged, O world?

Thoughts stirred by distant visions take root,
 custom and steadiness merge in a bond—
 though eyes dim, visions extend,
 do clarity and feeling persist, O world?

Without seeking grace or gain,
 devoted they work, day after day—
 If time forgets their quiet strength,
 does thyr worth fade, O world?

# Integrity and Character

When justice shifts the state's firm ground,
 it shreds half-born shame and fear;
 Integrity's glow that the world exalts—
 Isn't courage its root, O world?

Raised to bore burdens that fell again,
 enduring pain through endless time,
 who stood within trials' burning breath—
 do you sense their long ache, O world?

Those who hid truth amid constraint,
 can silence mean their truth was gone?
 Turning fire to calmest stream—
 do you see their radiant stand, O world?

They act as on a stage of speech;
 Is every actor truth's closure?
 Root-bruised, watching in silence still—
 do you perceive such grace, O world?

Are deeds that remember themselves forgotten—
 all earned honours fade with time;
 Yet when the unripe seed awakens in light,
 do you feel virtue bloom, O world?

# The Field of Memory

Wheels carved tales on earth's soft thread,
at turning edge, a story spread—
the shades aligned on life's long trail,
A field now deep where memories dwell.

Within the spinning wheel of heart,
each plunge renews a grace unseen,
eyes seek again that festive gleam—
A ground that grew into memory's dream.

On silver sand where weariness fades,
children danced in playful grace,
A drama bloomed where laughter swayed—
the field grew soft in time's embrace.

A gaze descends the well of care,
breaths hide where elders once stood near,
sound is born in depth of mind—
the field is blessed with golden air.

Rain brings moss and smiles anew,
parrots leap through glistening dew,
green carpets bloom, alive and true—
the field revived in nature's hue.

# Footprints of Friendship

Footprints mark the shadowed trail,
 A pattern grown on softened soil—
 where friendship's scepter made its mark,
 A blessing matured into fruitful treat.

In shadows came the star's soft gleam,
 eyes sparkling by the lantern's beam,
 fallen balls rolled like Ganges stream —
 A blessing grown in fulfilled dream.

Traces seek steady ground to roll,
 each bounce and step toward the goal,
 beyond the ball, no journeys lie—
 A blessing grown with meaning high.

Splashing up some laughter pearls,
 dropping cool green sprays like curls,
 deep scents in whispered words unfurl—
 A blessing grown as memories swirl.

On white sand strands of friendship lie,
 A boy forgets self in joyful try,
 among twelve friends, eyes dance and fly—
 A blessing united beneath the sky.

# The Scent of Changed Soil

In sparkling drops, the moonlight sways,
moving apart but still its own,
within the wheel's echoing tone,
the changed soil's breath finds its home.

A shower fell like a song that spilt,
dancing waves rose on sandy belt —
green imprints past frosted veil,
changed soil breathes a lively tale.

The southern corner's gentle sweep,
rain-dotted thorny grove so deep—
in deep abodes, the flood prevails,
changed soil tells memory's tales.

The breeze-lit candle in the heart,
stands firm where shifting paths part—
recalling lanes with clear sides bright,
changed soil breathes new glowing light.

At the edge of sight, a widening pond,
the turn that forgets its chosen bond—
cool shadows fold in joyful stay,
changed soil breathes a history's way.

# The Illumination of Virtue

In life's ever-shifting shaded fold,
love blooms as songs sung soft and bold—
wisdom stands resilient as silken thread,
supporting days though time has fled.

To mend life's complex twists with grace,
unchanging love and care embrace—
kinship strong that crosses shade,
A heart lights dark with bonds unfrayed.

Through feelings' path that blocks the night,
love shines forth in eyes bright,
steadfast truth and effort's glow,
kind words guide where virtues grow.

Perspective ripples wake intuition's flower,
words gilded in gold, an inner power,
like drops of rain in mental garden fair,
pure fragrance fills the mindful air.

Rain-danced mango leaves in breeze,
lightning's truth in words with ease,
A green river flows in humble tone—
A garland where sown grace shone.

# Shades of Stillness

Breeze drifts through mango groves' delight,
 we tore and tasted fruit half-bright,
 laughter spilled where sunlight played—
 the shade spun around like a tender top.

A falling drop on green's soft cloak,
 Surrounded by sky's eternal yoke,
 fragrant groves whisper in the air—
 light of faith an answered prayer.

Beauty fashioned like inner space—
 A tiny circle glowing in blue's embrace,
 softly sprouting petals, a silent conch;
 The piercing eye begins its stanch.

Without faith, it still will grow—
 no shrinking stem, no words too low.
 In youth, it holds a fervent green;
 Unseen paths of strength between.

A stone drops deep into the pool—
 our inner wheels spin and rule.
 Many ripples seek their way,
 awakening feelings that stray.

# Cloud-Shadow Memories

A faded blossom at the edge—
 its secret honour quietly shed;
 Time's feather brushes lightly on,
 A cloud drifts, memory's thread.

Even withered, spring lays her claim—
 faded flowers belong to the bloom.
 Closed recollections stir in the eye,
 beauty lingers in what we cannot touch.

Memories flowing like water's way—
 emerging, settling, scenes hold sway.
 Is knowing enough? We wonder still—
 An unknown spark ignites the thrill.

Some memories, filaments fine—
 call softly where feeling entwines;
 Turning in the trace less hush.
 Pain takes root as poetic verse aligns.

In dreams a mirror comes to view—
 revealing shapes in fleeting light;
 Imprinted voices echo true,
 time bends self to wider sight.

# Thought that Fell as Path

Like clouded dreams rooted deep,
  thoughts entwine like sugarcane sweet,
  though scattered, rhymes blend harmoniously—
  thoughts fall as paths of unity.

Formless forms in hands take shape,
  tools bloom into art and drape;
  Living breath in flowing cast,
  thoughts fall as shadows artfully vast.

Rootless gardens grow on air,
  free of weight, sights bare;
  Pearls bloom like rainless night,
  thoughts fall as newborn light.

One face gives paths anew,
  questions sprout from vantage view;
  Colours of carving curl in inner flight,
  thoughts fall like spirals bright.

Truth veiled like single light,
  sweet flavors clear and bright;
  Mind's eye opens where senses cease,
  thoughts fall where calm brings peace.

# Cycles of Knowing

Even a knot reflects a bud—
  each loop embraces whole as good,
  fullness found in every part,
  thoughts fall as patterns of heart.

Knotted words entwined with doubt,
  like enemies disguised about;
  Sharpness thrives in depths of pain,
  thoughts fall as questions that strain.

Steps lost to doubt now seek the true,
  tests leap out, the resolve anew;
  Fierce light praises wisdom bright,
  thoughts fall on paths challenging night.

Like a bee's hum on structured wings,
  even in buzzing, pure balance clings;
  Logic coaxes memory's way,
  thoughts fall in ordered ballet.

Linked essences wide in scope,
  systems grasp the greater hope;
  States spin down through valley's sweep,
  thoughts fall in cycles deep.

# The Path of the Journey

The journey starts with quietly seeking—
answers bloom as the heart goes roaming,
on green within the soul, bright wisdom grows,
the gift of walking is a goal ever unfolding.

With friends beside, the days move light,
laughter spills and words take flight,
the road ahead invites delight,
good company makes journeys bright.

Springtime stirs within the mind,
change arrives, leaves old ways behind,
new feelings blossom, quietly unfold—
gone amiss myself, now I grow bold.

Old memories walk the path I tread,
A sideways glance leaves blessings unsaid,
A few slow moments gather in the heart,
familiar sights that never depart.

Journeys of youth sow roots deep inside,
music of the new where old dreams reside,
in the end they settle, shaping who we are—
A life's direction, a guiding star.

# Changing Journeys

Thoughts foresee what lies ahead,
 experience drops where fears have tread,
 unexpected turns, though strange,
 add meaning deep within the range.

In search of self, the path rolls on,
 obstacles guide from dusk till dawn,
 the heart leaps high as anew it sees—
 wandering, wondering, never done.

New lessons dawn on the journey made,
 bridges found, and fears allayed,
 gifts and wisdom crowd the road,
 each step, a secret knowledge bestowed.

Crossing paths unseen, on the motion,
 both what passed and left in the ocean,
 joy and pain met within my eyes,
 like the wind, I will take flight and rise.

Emerging from shadows, new dawns arise,
 each step towards truth clears cloudy skies,
 the heart learns to dance with change and flow,
 in endless journeys, the self will grow.

# The Path of Renewal

Even the stillest, most hollow days—
  long dull, full of yearning lays—
  gave clarity, like a crystal's edge,
  shedding light into waking life.

I spun through seasons, tremors, change—
  burnt ground beneath my fleeting range.
  Each fall became a moving rise—
  every time reborn, a new road led me wise.

What seemed an ending, never really closed—
  from lesson's light arose the new blessed.
  Buds opened, smiling, in the next chamber—
  another door swung a new chapter.

Beneath many shadowed trees,
  memories trail and fade away —
  hidden as smoke drifting past sand,
  ancient paths continuing, unseen stand.

Each fallen seed puts down its root,
  across ages, sharp with truth—
  with fall and rise they thrive,
  every line of poetic mind sparks a life.